MONSTER
MUSICAL CHAIRS

by Stuart J. Murphy • illustrated by Scott Nash

HarperCollinsPublishers

To the fun-loving Robert Murphy family—
Bob and Ann,
Lee-Ann,
Melissa and Scott,
and Bryan
—S.J.M.

To Kyle and Sharon with love
—S.N.

The publisher and author would like to thank teachers Patricia Chase, Phyllis Goldman, and Patrick Hopfensperger for their help in making the math in MathStart just right for kids.

HarperCollins®, 🏠®, and MathStart® are registered trademarks of HarperCollins Publishers.
For more information about the MathStart series, write to HarperCollins Children's Books,
195 Broadway, New York, NY 10007. or visit our web site at www.harperchildrens.com.

Bugs incorporated in the MathStart series design were painted by Jon Buller.

Monster Musical Chairs

Library of Congress Cataloging-in-Publication Data
Murphy, Stuart J., 1942–
    Monster musical chairs / by Stuart J. Murphy ; illustrated by Scott Nash.
        p.   cm. — (MathStart)
    "Subtracting by one."
    "Level 1."
    Summary: As six monsters play a wild game of musical chairs, readers learn to subtract—one chair at a time.
    ISBN 0-06-028020-4. — ISBN 0-06-028021-2 (lib. bdg.).— ISBN 0-06-446730-9 (pbk.)
    1. Subtraction—Juvenile literature.   [1. Subtraction.]   I. Nash, Scott, 1959–   ill.   II. Title.   III. Series.
QA115.M872   2000   99-27902
513.2'12—dc21   CIP
                                                                                                                                AC

Typography by Elynn Cohen
20 EP 25 24
❖

MONSTER
MUSICAL CHAIRS

Smash-bash, BOOM. Clang-bang, CRASH!
The drums are pounding and the cymbals CLASH!

Everybody duck! Here come five chairs—
zig-zag-zipping through the air.

Hip-hip hooray! We're ready to play

MONSTER MUSICAL CHAIRS!

Six fuzzy monsters want a seat—
see them rock to a monster beat.

Five monster chairs all in a line.
Sit in one and you'll be fine!

Stomp stomp, SNORT. Shake shimmy, SHOUT!

When the music stops, one monster is OUT!

Good-bye, monster!

Five scary monsters left to play.
Now they throw one chair away.

Four monster chairs are still in place.
If you're not quick, you'll lose this race.

Stomp stomp, SNORT. Shake shimmy, SHOUT!

When the music stops, one monster is OUT!

So long, monster!

Four furry monsters growl and grin.
They can't wait for the band to begin.

Three monster chairs all in a row.
When the music starts, you can't be slow.

Stomp stomp, SNORT. Shake shimmy, SHOUT!

When the music stops, one monster is OUT!

See you later, monster!

Three hairy monsters left to play—
who will go and who will stay?

Two monster chairs still in the game.
If you're out now,

it'll be a shame.

Stomp stomp, SNORT. Shake shimmy, SHOUT!
When the music stops, one monster is OUT!

Bye-bye, monster!

Two monsters left. One place to sit.

There's just one winner—who'll be it?

Stomp stomp, SNORT. Shake shimmy, SPIN!
When the music stops . . .

One monster WINS!

If you lost this time, that's okay.
You can win this game another day.

31

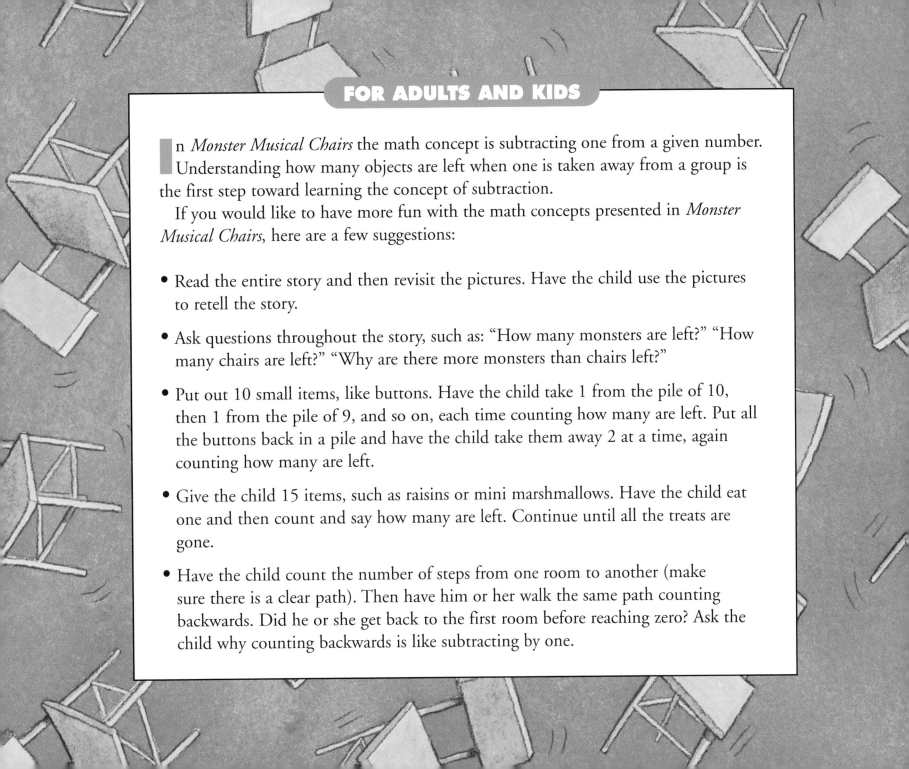

I n *Monster Musical Chairs* the math concept is subtracting one from a given number. Understanding how many objects are left when one is taken away from a group is the first step toward learning the concept of subtraction.

If you would like to have more fun with the math concepts presented in *Monster Musical Chairs*, here are a few suggestions:

- Read the entire story and then revisit the pictures. Have the child use the pictures to retell the story.

- Ask questions throughout the story, such as: "How many monsters are left?" "How many chairs are left?" "Why are there more monsters than chairs left?"

- Put out 10 small items, like buttons. Have the child take 1 from the pile of 10, then 1 from the pile of 9, and so on, each time counting how many are left. Put all the buttons back in a pile and have the child take them away 2 at a time, again counting how many are left.

- Give the child 15 items, such as raisins or mini marshmallows. Have the child eat one and then count and say how many are left. Continue until all the treats are gone.

- Have the child count the number of steps from one room to another (make sure there is a clear path). Then have him or her walk the same path counting backwards. Did he or she get back to the first room before reaching zero? Ask the child why counting backwards is like subtracting by one.

Following are some activities that will help you extend the concepts presented in *Monster Musical Chairs* into a child's everyday life.

Subtraction Concentration: You will need two players for this game. Number a set of index cards 1 through 10. Mix up the cards and lay them out facedown. The first player turns over a card. If it is 10, she keeps it and gets another turn. If not, the card is replaced and the second player gets a turn. Once the 10 is found, the players continue to look for 9, 8, 7, etc. When 1 is found, the game is over. The player with the most cards wins.

At the Store: Before you check out, together count the number of items in the grocery cart. As you or the child places the items on the checkout counter, ask how many are left in the cart.

Around the Kitchen: After dinner, have the child count the number of utensils on the table. As the child clears the table, talk about how many remain on the table.

The following books include some of the same concepts that are presented in *Monster Musical Chairs*:

- TEN, NINE, EIGHT by Molly Bang

- SPLASH by Ann Jonas

- SIX BRAVE EXPLORERS by Kees Morbeck and Carla Dijs